Planet Middle Age

Gerry Potter

Flapjack Press
www.flapjackpress.co.uk

First published in 2010 by Flapjack Press
6 Chiffon Way, Trinity Riverside, Gtr Manchester M3 6AB
www.flapjackpress.co.uk

ISBN-13: 978 0 9555092 7 8

Facebook: Gerry Potter-Poet
MySpace: gerrypotterpoet

Cover design by Brink
www.mucusart.co.uk
All images taken from Facebook
with kind permission of the photographers

Printed & bound in Great Britain by Direct-POD
Saxon Fields, Old Harborough Road, Brixworth, Northampton NN6 9BX
www.direct-pod.com

To Shaun,
a brilliant mind, a wonderful man and me Fittie Chuckleys.
I love you.
G x

Contents

Star
by Pam Leeson

last words whisper
a silent giggle thunders by
grins out loud

the rainbow's end sings
a last time lullaby

he's awake to a new planet
the prince of seven

waltzing with now
tracing jigs of long gone

a piece of memory
curls around the new day

be prepared

to parlez with danger
clear as disaster
it beckons you over

watch for a house
winking you in
welcome, wipe your feet

be prepared to laugh

shelves of happy hold cups
of salt water, disguised
as something to swim in

dismiss a first glance

look for words hidden
down the back of the settee

be prepared for love
in every other room

gather round yesterday
its smile holds you hostage

be prepared for love

gallop upstairs
for an after dinner fuck

fall to the floor
waterfall oblivion

be prepared to cry

there's more in the cellar
more than you think
there could be

keep your mouth away
from your eyes away
from your soul

and something else will
creep in

ignore everything
something else will happen

this planet is his button
the universe,
the hole it fits into.

Middle-Aged Spread

Episode IV: An Adventure In Time And Space

The Story Teller's dreams are a flurry of time travel and distraction. One minute he's somewhere, next minute somewhere else. He doesn't know whether he's been there before or, indeed, just arrived. So many stories and lifetimes lived, loved and squandered, not just his own. Can't help burrowing into the core of memories. Gets confused, wondering if it's his memory or someone else's, then contents himself with the memory of memories.

Right now he's happy not making sense. Sitting at the corner of a cloud fishing for raindrops then guffawing with donkeys at a kindergarten pantomime, elegant with surrealism. Takes time out to wonder when he'll wake then jumps in the fire counting pearls. The flames are blue and compliment his eyes, all twenty-five of them. Here, there's a party of poets and drunks dancing wayward and waving dogma at God. The bunting brittles melodies of famous battles and tin-whistles its way to the loo. The tin-whistles join a one-man band and air guitar medley of Wagner and ABBA. Julie Covington sings the lead.

All the girls decide they're boys and then the boys dress as girls; they ask each other out for dinner and waspishly dine on the winter of discontent. There are berries made of hiccups and wine distilled from tears. The running buffet hops, skips and jumps into spring, and daffodils speak Scouse. Music barnstorms the heavens with a trumpeting of occasions and flounders in the sea, doggy-paddling with aplomb. The catfish bite back and mew a daytime soap starring all his friends. There's a jostling for position and the star on his dressing room door is made of chocolate.

There's no end to the extra-curricular activity of dreams the Story Teller trills, as he blunders through childhood, excavating the antiques of adults.

*

Middle age and all our dreams should be golden. I'm writing this and very soon I shall be forty-eight. I'll be honest, it makes me gasp. It's not that I fear ageing, it's just being forty-eight. That's nearly fifty years on this planet and, when you break it down, that's a lot of harrowing hours and merry minuets.

For huge chunks of my life I've been a full-blown hedonist, not really caring what's round the corner just as long as I have a good time getting there. I believe in hedonism, in the freedom of the spirit, the adventuring of the soul. I'll be very honest, the times they are a-changing and I am now starting to believe in the hedonism of slowing down.

This book is an act of creative hedonism and has taken six months to write, from inception until now. I wanted a fast representation of how I'm feeling at, and in, this very moment.

All the poems bar one are of the moment. And that moment is my middle age.

A lot has happened in the year since my last book, *Planet Young*. A lot of it - not all - has made it into here. There are still stories on the boil and not ready to pour; they're not yet memories. I find memories easier to write, they're malleable, not as stubborn as *now*. This book is a catalogue of memories recently exhumed and brought back to life. I love the Frankenstinean power of being a writer. A robber of my own grave experiences. Not everything in here is grave, but I'm no longer afraid of the dark.

Being a writer and its mouldy old responsibilities *sigh*. I love it, but, blimey, it can sometimes weigh you down. I thank the Seven Seas and all their salt I'm not as hung up on it as other writers seem to be. Writing for me is a tricky beast because I hardly read, so there's never anything to measure it against. Not for me the constant rewriting and revision. I'm all for it, if that's your ball, but I like the accidental splendour of the splash. Of course, I've reviewed and reworked some of the poems in here, but not to within an inch of their lives. Like with all birth, I feel you should try and get used to what you've got, rather than painstakingly shape it into your own image. I think I'd be a great parent.

I've been asking friends how they feel about being middle-aged and the range of answers has been extraordinary, from abject fear and denial to all-embracing certainty. Of course, there are friends who are physically fitter than others, but they are not necessarily the ones handling it the best. A lot of my friends are disco damaged. Some are still dancing, others are not. Reading through these poems has brought home just how profound an effect partying has had on my life. I've done many things, some of them would be considered major achievements, but nothing comes close to simply loving having a good time. I've had moments of love, laughter and dancing that will live on much longer than any written word. As I trawl through experience and life, I'm aware of that more. You really can't write down a smile or a dance, you have to do it. Saying that, I hope you feel the deep throb of techno and the heartbeat of its bass in some of the work.

I want you to read these poems with brio and passion. I want you to dance with them. They come from my heart and the performance that pumps in there. They are hedonist, even when they seem not to be. Free verse troubadours and gypsies, raw with verve and colour. They're from a history of camp and movement, both profound and silly. All our lives are larger than life if we want them to be, but we've got to want them to be, and if you don't want them to be, that's cool.

Middle age and its moseying creepery. It's such a sneaker-upper, sure it wears slippers. If I have a problem with it, then it's vanity: while I have no problem with the actual years I've spent on this planet, I wish I still had hair. I loved my leonine mane. It's odd, I never realised how vain I was until now. Looking back on old photos I think, *Hey kid, you were sitting on a fortune.* I now know I look older and it's an ok problem. It hurts, but I can deal with it.

It doesn't help when people say fifty is the new forty. It isn't! I look back at photos of me forty and there's a huge difference. I despise that kind of unintellectual positivia. For me, the only way forward is to face the facts. That way, you're dealing with the actuality, not the myth.

Middle age is an ongoing saga, dripping in the potency of now, of right now. What happens when we stop being middle-aged and when does that stopping start? If we move the goalposts forever we'll ruin the game. The great big question is where from here? My generation of eternal teenagers are going to make fascinating geriatrics, as pompous and eccentric as Margaret Rutherford and James Robertson-Justice, I hope. More of that when it happens and, if I'm around, I shall most definitely document it. *Planet Middle Age: Part II* or will it be *Planet Old*?

The one thing I know is that I shall be living it, no matter how many days, months, or years I have left. I suggest you do, too. It's not old that makes you 'Old', it's inactivity. So get out there and give it the ongoing blast of your punk breathlessness. Beat your chest and, while you're loosening your catarrh, primal scream demands from the world around you. Don't stop telling stories, but don't stop making them either. You're middle-aged now and, yes, you're getting older, but there's a bitch in the old dog yet.

We often talk of 'Wisdom of the Ancients' and how wonderful and rich that is. Perhaps middle age is us becoming junior ancients and we're on our way to some beautiful vein of being. Perhaps not. Perhaps it's up to us.

Before you start toddling to your grave in a Zimmer frame, give a thought to just how genuinely young middle age is right now.

*

"C'mon, Gerard!"

The Story Teller wakes with a start and realises he's tired; even sleep was full of ideas and experience. The long journey of adventuring and long adventuring of dreaming has taken its toll. The jungle is in night and scented stock is taking a becalming effect. The moon is lullabying in tune and melodic. He feels heady and sunburned, like he's spent all day at the seaside and now it's time for the train home. Sand between toes. The friction of a good time.

He gives the space-chair a friendly pat and climbs inside. He initialises the controls and is almost ready for take off. Before pressing the big red shiny button he muses on recent events: saving the earth from itself; taking on dinosaurs; reconnecting with his grandmother - all in a day's work. He giggles with superhero satisfaction and really must do it again sometime.

He likes it here but over there, beyond the forest, there's a very real world to contend with, and school tomorrow. The horror of P.E., scarier than Christopher Lee. Anyway, he has to get back to send his mother to sleep. He's sure he has enough stories.

The dome of the space-chair closes. Everything is in position for take off. Takes a last slurp of dandelion and burdock, a bite of Topic, and presses the big red shiny button.

The End

Planet Middle Age

Blank

This is how some middle-aged friends get drunk.

Starts like it always starts,
Blank.
Without thought.
Moseys its way to somewhere
Then whiskey.
There's ice,
A reassuring clink clink.
A scent of stories.
The Wild West,
Hand-painted tepees,
A soporific cavalry,
Or something Eastern to do with spies.
The Orient Express slows down,
A sputtered echo of train tracks.
Your poison takes hold
And at last you're able to breathe.
The first intake of breath
And the rest is history.

You're sat,
The outside world
Loses its grip.
Fingernails on glass,
Screeching,
Crushing to velvet.
It's slow.
There's distorted pillow talk.
"On your own," the voice speaks.

Down down deeper and down.
See yourself on the horizon.
The cavalry's woken,

Looking like a welcome tale
And now it's safe to sigh.
Hic!
You're smiling, blurred and fudged,
At the fairground mirrors of nonchalance.

And the armchair wraps around
Like a lover should.

Visions Of A Holy Isle

In my middle age I've been annually retreating with a group of writers to the magnificent Isle of Arran. On the Isle of Arran, opposite the shore of Lamlash, is the Holy Island. The Holy Island has been bought by a Buddhist sect. It is a wonderful place, eerie as tender.

My unromantic says
It's just a mossy cowpat
Afloat in a moat of bull-piss
And rain.
A bovine relic, steaming,
Pregnant with untold histories
Of miscarried pauses.
Well passed its sell by date.
Well past.
Boring as the day is long.

It's miss and miss.
Shit-mist.
Mist-shaped.
A flat brown winter of waste
Imbued with all the mystery of a fart.
The bubbling insignificance of a forgotten
Pop tune,
A dwarf letter in the page-churning
Rant of history,
Lit for an unremarkable second
By the erratic wink of a dyslexic lighthouse,
Blind in one eye.

My unromantic
Sits in a tower block, miserable
Of cider cider cider
And a mule-headed jigsaw of the war.
He's the enemy attacking his honey

Whose arsenal is depleted of money,
And there's always one piece missing,
And the missing piece
Is peace.

My romantic
Hails it as a lump of God,
Holds it aloft.
Earth chalice.
Basks in its sunshine.
Holier than holy,
But not holier than thou
Or thine.
A place where rest can admit it's tired,
Holiday,
Recharge its batteries
So it can carry on working.

Gives peace a chance to recover from war,
Stories the playtime freedom of children
In its hip hip hooray grassy catacombs.

The Buddhists:
Silent punctuation,
Orange and yellow full stops,
Commas and apostrophes.

My romantic hand in hands
With the lighthouse,
Who circles my marriage finger
In a bright ring of water.
The lighthouse is a gentleman
Tipping a nod,
Picking up my handkerchief.

"Gonna marry that lighthouse,"
My romantic says,

"And honeymoon like the Owl and the Pussycat
On the carefree blessed amber
Of this shore."

My romantic smiles with the dawn,
Nods in weary agreement with the dusk.

In My In Me

Due to popular demand here's my coming out poem. I'm glad I've written it now, not then, as I normally hate coming out poems. It's set the day after the night I went to Liverpool's The Masquerade, Masque, or The Mazzie. My first gay club. A legendary nightclub, no longer in corporeal existence, but alive and vibrant in the minds of the middle-aged, elderly and, of course, the dead.

In my in me,
Corridors,
Long,
Smeared,
White.
Words are
Blood red graffiti.
There's a monster carnival
Roaring for approval.

Summer's
A
Twisting
Animal.

Bleating pop tunes,
The best pop tunes,
And the same old,
Same old,
Nursery rhymes.

Horror stories
Of success
Stick
And its endless lists of failure
Scare.

Gawky,
Slapped,
Stripped.

There's a child not hearing children
Hearing children
Laughing,
Playing and laughing.
In my in me,
Sound,
Traces of comfort,
Bread for pigeons,
Monologues for teachers.

The trains are fast.
Dust
Evolves,
Revolves,
Carries a crisp packet.
A salt 'n' vinegar twister
Unable to whisk me away.

River calm,
Swim less,
City centre a family.
Walking punctuates
The sentence,
Makes words of the pavement,
Colours of the fruit barrow
A rainbow.
The woman shouting carrots
A goddess,
A banshee.
Take your pick.

Traffic,
Newspapers,

Buses,
Chips.

The shape of theatres
Softer than churches.
Knelt,
Erect,
Confessing.

I fancy Tom Jones
And Peter Purves.
Where I come from it's wrong to fancy
Peter Purves.
In my in me,
Touching
Bliss,
Shitting bricks.
Bless.

The bookshop's
Thinking
Pages,
It senses stories.
Aroma thought,
Smell knowledge.

People I don't know.
Guilt weighs
Small change,
Quiet,
Still.
In my in me,
War.

Night sky
Streaked red.
Sun down,

Eyes wide.

Chewing gum,
Damp floor,
Sticky prayers.
A tiny cathedral.

I met queers last night,
They were dancing
Such dances.
Nuclear,
Unclear,
Strong.

Our Paul
1952-2006

When I was a kid I had the best older brother. Cheeky and raw. Fearless and wayward. A stereotypical comedic scamp. A dead-end kid, alive with the sense of misadventure. A truth-stretcher like no other. Our Paul crystallises the nostalgia of my childhood and the grief of middle age.

This is not definitely a lie,
But most certainly the truth.
It's our Paul,
And lies
Somewhere between
Feeling
And sometimes.

There are stories so great
They can't be told,
Stories so told they
Can't be great,
It's where cliché and imagining live.
Our Paul
Lived somewhere there and somewhere else,
In-between.
A place of schemes,
Of parties without end,
Children's daydreams.

Was as real as he could make it.
Couldn't make it real sometimes.

There are stories so sad
They must not be shared,
Truth so fragile it sounds like lies,
So complicated it can't be said.
Heart-twisting.

Our Paul
Had endeavour,
His head the Himalayas,
The Dark Side of the Moon.
Pink Floyd,
Pink Fairies
And '70s LSD.

Ugly cute.
Lithe as a footballer.
Taught me to rip off doors for bonfire wood
And how to laugh without embarrassment.
Kids wanted his humour and sweets,
The Pied Piper of Blackstock Street.
Had Southport in his pockets,
New Brighton in his eyes.

The police took him away once
When I was six.
I ran
After the car.
It broke my heart.

Our Paul
Had the monopoly on ragamuffin,
On *honest to God* and *sumthin'*.
The first scally.
Rough and tumble,
Unreliable as dice.

Our Paul
Worked in a factory,
But wanted to take over the world.
Had the plans.
He was a super villain,
The police didn't stand a chance.
It was all about him,

The family
And the working class.
Oh yeah, we all shared in his dream.
Our Paul
Dreamt the first dream.

He looked of the time.
Face like a bust watch,
Nickname was Butch once,
Hair like Marc Bolan's.
We spun our Spider-Man moments.
Said he was proud of me,
Gave me pocket money
And cried at sad things.
Troubled youth.
Our Paul
Ran rings round police
And truth.

Knew he was a hero,
Had that look.
Anarchy,
Warmth
And the trust of kids.
Played it, and football, brilliantly.

Honest!

Honest to God.

It's what I need to remember.

Mary Mac
1944-2009

Mary Mac was really Mary Butler, my sister-in-law. We called her Mary Mac cos McMahon was her maiden name. It's a Scouse thing. Sometimes it's not until someone dies that you realise just how important a figurehead they were in your history. Mary Mac was a huge influence on my life. This is a tribute to her and women like her.

Mary
Oh Mary
Mary Mac
You know we want you back
Mary
Oh Mary . . .

Read these women
Built from war.
Diamonds cut from fighting,
Liverpool and water.
Salt-river pearls
Shaped my world.
Mersey-maids.
The sound of sirens singing down-town shanties
Gave me the true feel of right and wrong,
Steel and song.

I watched Mary Mac graft a family
With our John,
A low wage
And the misunderstood rage of
A mother.
All those sons
Bawlin' an' roarin'
Almost every day against the tide.
Her sense of humour,

Concrete.
Feather-light and industrial,
Jimmy Mac and musical,
Tar-Mac and unusual.

Mary Mac made me gasp
And spent money,
Not knowing where the next penny
Was coming from.
Made curry macaroni
From a secret recipe of . . .
She preferred curry macaroni
To scouse.

Made her own rice pudding
Even though she could have bought a tin.

Mary Mac took me to school for the first time
Because my mother couldn't.
Helped me make
My Holy Communion.
I remember that mustard cardigan
Made me feel old,
I'm sure she picked it.

She used to work in a sweet shop.
I'd annoy her.
She said I was too choosy,
Could never make my mind up.
Once shooed me out.
God, she had a temper,
Shriek of a hell-cat, I remember.

That night with Kathleen Gregory,
Our Janet,
Our Cathy,
And me mum.

Women and me.
I made so many cups of tea,
Boiled ham sandwiches and biscuits.
Stories of dead loved ones,
Thomas and Jimmy,
Of old neighbours.
Mary Mac and Kathleen had me doubled up.
It's the only time I've genuinely pissed myself laughing.

Mary Mac's beehive is my earliest memory.
'60s.
Three.
Hard and soft like Tara King's,
The smell of that particular lacquer.
The '60s and our John's still a Teddy Boy.
It'll soon be the '70s and our John will still be a Teddy Boy.
The mirror that turned into a picture of Gethsemane,
The holy picture.
Magic.

Mary Mac changed with the decades,
But should've been filmed in black and white,
Been written by a playwright.
Could tell stories,
Brilliant stories.
She'd watch us play Cowboys and Indians.
The Last of the McMahon's.
Swore like a trooper,
Believed in prayer.

Mary Mac had Christmas sewn up.
I remember the excitement of the big Kwik Save shop,
And how could one woman carry so many selection boxes?
Mary Mac could.
She grew arms,
Was Shiva sometimes.
Became Queen of Grandkids.

Mrs Christmas.
She suffered fools never
And worried.
I remember her looking at my dead mother and saying,
"But May, who'll pay the Provvy Man?"

Mary Mac took us to the Pier Head on Sunday afternoons,
Bottles of lemonade and sugar butties.
Loved the sound of kids laughing.
Fizzy kids.
Was brave.
Hard.
Loved our John.
Sang and danced 'Achy Breaky Heart' to him
Like a Vaudevillian.
Knees up skirt up ooh la la,
The Mary Mac Follies.
Loved her whiskey
And her ciggies.
I wished I'd kissed her goodbye.

These women,
Forgotten books
Collecting dust in libraries of achievement,
Are, and have always been,
History you'll never read about.

Mary
Oh Mary
Mary Mac
You know we want you back
Mary
Oh Mary.

Mr Feast Face

If you stand up wind
He niffs of sausage rolls and all-sorts,
Liquorice and pork.
The people who inhabit the bus stop
Spend a long time imagining he's not there.

His hair a chewing gum sticky fondant
Of lice and confetti crisps.
Ice-cream greens his nose,
Mint choc chips.

Chomps on air,
Tastes the malice
And baulks on the flippant fancies of people.
Mr Feast Face slurps and drools.

Stares erotically at pigeons.
I fancy he fancies a pie.
Feathers don't choke Mr Feast Face,
They tickle his throat,
Electric trickle.
He giggles
And trumpets sweet things at the sour.
Bubbles sad stories.
Dark chocolates.
There was that film when no-one believed
He was Santa Claus.
He tells anyone anything.
I fancy he fancies
Me.

Remembers burnt Sunday dinners,
His mum's rhubarb pie,
The foreboding pinny of his grandmother.

If you stand up wind you can hear her crow.
You'll probably blame a bird.

Mr Feast Face moans.
He's all out of all-sorts.

His grandmother the rolling pin.
Mother's miss-shapes.
Crackers.

His father
Scone.

The Witherers

I firmly believe some people don't have souls and they are after yours . . .

Pokey dark fingery
Thingery,
Spindly men and women,
Woodcuttings and real.

They stand, corner stood,
Whittling maggots from tears.
Stand, corner stood,
Stealing twinkles
From eyes,
Leaving you dimly lit with malady,
Blights and monsters.
Beware The Witherers,
Their disguises,
Sometimes they look like
Friends.

Witherers hover
Two inches outside your window.
Echo-tap footsteps
Pollute your dreams,
Steal beauty sleep,
Stuff it in jars
And a-down they go,
A-withering,
A-quivering,
A-selling it in pubs for a fiver.

Dark they go,
Seeping,
Sagging,
Slobbering the putrid of drains.

Beware The Witherers,
Their disguises,
Sometimes they look like
Family.
Down they go,
Working underground and overtime,
Creeping around the graveyard shift.
Check your mother's fingernails
For coffin splinters,
Check her breath for a rose scent,
A lily breeze,
Her purse for the acquisitive
Scuffed souls of children.

Never let them tell you secrets.
A Witherer's secret could steal your soul,
Make you murder your angel.
"Snap her wings, garrotte her with her halo,
Rip out her feathers,"
They rasp,
Whisper tinny.
Witherers have, and will always hate,
The potential of wings.

The Witherer will sell you your heartbeat,
Read the untellable in your mind
And broadcast it to the world.
They'll invisible in the corner,
Staring at your favourite chair.
That chill that grabs your spine?
A Witherer's stare, that is.
Dark they go.

Beware The Witherers,
Their disguises,
Sometimes they take on your features.
Sometimes take on your futures.

Sometimes they look like your furniture.
A lumpy cushion could house a Witherer's knees.
Witherers have knobbly needs.

Never join a Witherer's song,
Their melodies maim.
It's the howl in your pipes
Calling your name,
An owl song sung by a demon.

Witherers thirst for, and feast on, the last death rattle,
The almost of breath.
Nibble at grief,
Bleed bad medicine,
Slow poison,
Exalt mediocre
And dark they go.
Beware The Witherers,
Their disguises,
Sometimes they look like your doctor.

If you see a Witherer in the sliver of a mirror
Nod your head three times,
Touch your heart, and say
Love.

Folly Butler And The Ninety-Nine Soldiers Of Death

Folly Butler is a dream person, an amorphous character, a thought muse. She exists in my subconscious. She's a gift to write for because anything could happen to her. Folly first popped up in my previous book Planet Young *and I think will follow me for quite some time.*

Folly Butler
Stood a-top the world
In lily slippers
And an apron wove from bliss,
Her first born
Nestled closely to her breast.
She sings a lullaby in daffodil,
Alma Coganesque.
It falls like blossom,
Leaving her child's skin singing gentle.
Singing protected.
Singing blue skies.
Singing sleep.

Here, in the haze of daydreams,
Her silhouette,
A pillow.

Folly Butler
And her ninety-nine babies
Etched on the same saucers as Winnie the Pooh,
As Jemima Puddleduck,
As The Candy-Floss Bobbins of Pluto,
As Rupert the Bear.

Stood a-top the world with her first born,
Whispers to God of fulfilment
And how proud she is of nature.
Folly Butler,

Heart of light
And forgiveness,
Sinks into the delicious sound of comfort.

And then the soldiers came.

Tramp Tramp
Smash Smash
Kill Kill
Tramp Tramp
Smash Smash
Kill Kill.
Shock and Awe.
I have no poetry for this.

Folly Butler,
No longer a mother.
The enemy!
A deceitful whore,
Cunt full of maggots,
Mouth full of lies,
The killer of children.
Her God a conspirator.
Her time on Earth
A waste of time.

Etched in her soul,
The Jack of the Ripper,
The Moors of the Murderers,
Ra Ra Rasputin
And the end of democracy.
Folly Butler and her children
Must die.

The ninety-nine soldiers of death,
Eyes cold as celebrities singin' Christmas.
Peace-keeping baby sitters

Asleep in the blood of innocents,
Heavy with the rape of calm,
Hard as the cold of stone.
Some of them laughing.

Folly Butler
Points to God,
Crying.
They had once been babies.

Folly Butler And The Ghosts Of The Dead

By the Mersey,
Hardly standing,
Weeping the river.
Looking,
Not seeing the distance.
Her grief further than the sun,
Close as its reflection.
All her tears
Burning.
Her skin brown paper,
Cheeks burning.

Mouth
Hollow as a tunnel,
Sound
Clear as drowned.
The noise of howling.
Haunting.

Echoes
Of her slaughtered
Wash against the pier.
Spray her face.
Wretch of the wind,
Splinter wet.

There is no-one in this.
She is nothing.
Past tense
Of a mother.
A name called by mouths
Not there.
Not hungry.

She is pointing.

Turns to her husband.
He is a spiller of salt,
Drunk,
A weed of a man
Distilled from tears.

A woman in a red scarf reassures,
"They are little stars in the sky,
No-one can touch them now."

Folly Butler wants them back,
Jealous of the sky.

Folly Butler And The Life Of Death

Overwhelmed,
The crash of water walls,
Gulping like sobbing.
"Oh my God, she's in the river!"
A swoosh of panic bouncing.
Soft
Loud
Loud
Soft.
Save her!
"Save her!"
Soft
Loud
Screams,
Gulls between waves,
Stereo of bubbles and noise.
The pitch of panic.
Save her!
"My God, will someone save her!"

Folly Butler
Dives.
Reaching,
Grabbing,
Not panicking,
Not drowning.
Ninety-nine babies cheer her on.
River voices,
Water chorus.
The soldiers won't get her this time.
Dives.
The smash of calm
As she stretches,
Dank weights of water as she lunges down.

She grabs the sinking bundle.
Coming up for air,
Reaching for the sun,
The break of surface,
Relief of breath.
Kiss of life.

A sobbing mother takes her child,
Stunned father wraps his coat.
Folly Butler stands drenched,
Alone,
Summer-wet and sagging.

The crowd around her
Ticker-tape applause.
The sound around her like bullets.
The flash of memories like cameras.
The names of every one of her children strobing.
The not knowing.

The mother says,
"Thank you thank you thank you,
You've just saved my child.
If there's anything I can do . . ."
Folly Butler answers in daffodil,
"Tirripel miret plook bista
Ogla hooth smerriten scheep."
Which means,
"Please may I have your baby?"

She is pointing.

Pantomimeism

I've steered clear for far too long. I just had to write a poem drama about Capitalism gone mad. I thought as I got older it would get better. It hasn't.

The Big Bad Wolf, a feral hero who fights for the injusticed people of Pantoland, is stopped in her paws by the wicked Granny who has another way for the Pantolanders to live their lives. We start our tale after Granny, with the help of the Woodcutter, fooled the Big Bad Wolf into drinking their wicked transformative concoction. The Big Bad Wolf starts to visibly crack open and change, much to the horror of her lover, Simple Simon, who can only watch helplessly on.

Crriiiick ttkkkct
Crrraaaaacckkkkkkkkkk.
Crick
Crick
Rrrrriiiiiiiiiiiiiiipppppp.
Streeeettttetchhhhhhhhhh!!!!!!

"Oh, it's huge,"
Granny honked.
"Huge, dark and loaded.
Splintering,
Bourgeoning,
Bigger than the night sky.
Look, Simon.
Bloated head brain burst,
The rip of flesh,
A cataclysm of skin and bone.
I'm no longer alone."

Aaaaaaaaggghhhhrraaaahhhhhh!!! Heelllpppp meeee . . . . . .

"Metamorph!"
Spat Granny,

Bored of its hairy arse, ivory teeth and cobalt eyes.
"Grow, devour and complicate.
Decimate,
Slaver pools of acid water.
Rank up injustice,
Jaundice wealth.
Find a broken prisoner
Or a recently deceased pensioner,
Open its mouth
And piss in it."

Scriiiiicettttchhhhhhh grrrrrrowellllllll!!!

"Disembowel,"
Murmured the Woodcutter, exhausted.
"What's good for the goose is sauce for the gander.
Roll up roll up roll up,
Take a moment.
Take a tenner.
Take a gander at the murdered goose,
Mother of all geese."
He smiles wooden teeth,
Coughs,
Splutters woodworm,
Fries and sells golden eggs.

Reeeeaaarrrrrghhhhh pleeeease stop this pleeaaaaassseee!!!

"There there there, don't cry now,"
Granny reassured the wolf.
"So nearly there.
Take a look, Simple Simon,
Look what's left of your lover.
A new world order,
A flea-bitten extra of awkward theatre.
Awkward but simple.
So simple, Simon,

Even you can be king
Of somewhere,
Of something.
A kingdom of everything you could ever buy or dream.
You never thought yourself a dreamer, had you, Simon?"

Simple Simon knelt weeping,
Gagged,
Chain-bound.
A pie-man dabs his lips with the last drops of water.

Strrreettherscriiiiip arrrrarhghhhh eeearrraaaaaghhh
No no no stop it,
Stop! Stoooopppp iiiittttttttttt
Stoooooooop iiiiiiiiiiiiiiiiiiiiiiiiiiieeearrrrgh please stop it!!!

"No!"
Roared Granny, pinny on fire,
Rolling pin erect.
"There have been too many tears.
Where there is discord, let us bring harmony;
Confusion, let us bring clarity.
Where there is despair, stand up comedy;
Hair, let us bring hairspray.
Where there is starving, let us bring charity;
Where there are saints, let us bring Bono;
Where there is *oh yes,*
Let us bring *oh no.*
Crisis, what crisis?
Where there's crisis, let us bring television.
And where there is television, let us bring
Pantomimeism.
Let the world engorge on Pantomimeism.
We're behind you.
Oh no we're not.
Switch on.
We're in front of you.

Ha ha ha ha haaa haaaa haaaaaaaa!"

***Eeeeeraaaarrreeeyaaaaaaaaaaaaaaa arrgh help meee!
Maaaaake it stop maaaaaaaaaaaaaaakkke iiiiiitttt
Stoooooooooooooooooooooop! Maaake iit stttoooop!!!***

"Impossible!"
Bellowed Grandma.
"You, my sweet, have the power to set us free.
I am nurture,
You are nature.
You are we.
With you at my heels, we will conquer
And share picklets plucked from ravages of time,
Feast off scavengers.
With the Rage by my side
We will decorate this world a golden porn,
Make it tattle lullabies of vicious tittle while it sleeps, dead.
Make the feral think they're cool,
The ineffectual, intellectual.
Come my Rage, come,
Be whole and emancipate,
Be whole and disintegrate
The favoured and the meek.
Emasculate,
Emaciate.
Fuck them my Rage,
Fuck them mercilessly."

***Eeeeeeeeeeeaaaaaarrrrrrrghhhhhhhhh. Noooooooooooo.
Must stop thiiis. Musssst stoooop thiiissss!***

"No!"
Roared Granny.

***Must stop this . . .
Eeeeearrrrggthraaawpppaaaaaaaaaaaaaaaaahhhhhhhhhh!***

Wroooooong aaaaaallll wrong. No noooooooooooooooooo!!!!!!

"Too late, too late,"
Granny gloated,
"It's done.
Good Hades, it's done.
One last push,
This labour is soooo working.
That's it.
Done.
Over at last.
Sooooo over.
Oh bliss.
The bliss of this.
Time for change.
There you are, my emergent.
Thrilling.
Can't contain myself.
Couldn't contain yourself.
At last,
Pretty.
Awful ordeal over, my liddle baby.
Big Bad gone for good.
Come Goldie,
Glitter next to Granny.
There there my pretty,
So pretty.
Pink the colour of flesh,
The almost colour of blood,
All fashioned in rows and rows
Of gingham ribbons and bows.
Oh goody goody good.
Smile those smiles,
The ones we rehearsed,
Like a child.
No fangs dear, no fangs,
Never give the game away,

Remember the punter's always right.
Forget the night,
It's forever daylight now.
Oh look my dear, the Woodcutter's drooling sawdust
For us.
Shan't waste it.
We'll use it for breath.
Look at you, so fully emerged,
Pussed, poised and hooded red,
With all the puff puff skin of a soap cherub.
Rest the tranquil of angels,
Bask in the sigh of the ageless.
What big pound signs you have.
All the better to sell me with, my dear.
The monochrome of the depthless awaits and welcomes,
Oh, how it welcomes.
Pretty,
So pretty.
My angel, so Goldilocked and lilac-eyed.
Perfect for a single tear.
You will weep pearls,
I promise.
How peaceful you look, my velveteen baby,
In your svelte red cloak
And goody two shoes
Crafted from the leather of a debtor's tongue.
Little Miss Jimmy Choos,
Dorothy will be soooo jealous.
Such style, such sighs.
Such lies, why even I may blush.

"What a shame . . .
Simple Simon's died.

"Oh my pretty, with your basket empty,
Fill it with baubles, bangles
And the beady sweat of diamond miners.

Make the empty grovel
So you can feed
And fill
And fill
And fill
And fill
And fill
And fill
And fill
And fill
And fill
And fill
And fill
And fill
And fill
And fill
And fill
And fill
And fill
Fill and stay pretty.
Pretty for the ugly.
Feed my pretty,
Feed,
Remember you're doing them a favour,
Feeeeeeeeeeeeed!
You're what the ugly need."

The Woodcutter collects
Skin and bones
And what's left of Simple Simon's belongings.
"It'll sell well on eBay,"
He drizzles.

And they all lived enormously ever afterwards.

Auntie Matter

The woman sat next to me
Is an alien.
She points in tentacles,
Accuses me of laughing at the world.
She mind probes my head,
A quarry.
Stumbles among the remnants of memory and adventure.

I see through her visor of smoked glass and excuses.
She hides vodka in the cistern,
Chides her children for being.
Hates humanity,
Supports the system.
A shrike as she weeps,
The detritus of apology.
Makes me ache.
Want to send her home.
Find her a space-bus
And pay the fare.

I want her to know what planet she lives on,
I want her to know a planet she can love on
And share
Her vodka and ideas.
I'm pretty sure she has ideas.

A ray gun pointing,
Wants to disintegrate.
Has given birth to a family
She wants to exterminate.
Dalek-Mother,
Cyber-Gran,
Living nanoseconds too long.
Psyche in hyperspace,

Rage in hyper-face,
Auntie Matter
Doesn't matter.
No more important than a quiz show.

ZAP!
Positive-Negative.
ZZZRRRIIIIPPPPPIITTTT!

Looks like she's never known love.

Thirty-Six Hours

This is about one of my last blasts of unbridled hedonism. A two week bender. It's about E, booze and whatever I could get my hands on. It's also about reawakening to the idea of love, the love of a good man, good times and great drugs. Dedicated to that shiver of night we can all slip through.

Oh come on!
So much booze and E in my veins,
A blur of futures passin'.
Inner-city blues of a night well hung,
Ablaze with white noise and dance.
Tonight I'm gonna fall in love,
Promise I'm gonna fall in love,
And it's gonna change the world.

Up in the air with a million hookers,
So personal and free.
Eyes bored of all we've seen.
Pretty sure we're all whores.

Maybe tonight we'll all fall in love,
Joke with a million punch lines.
Joke I've told
A million and one times.
Maybe tonight we'll see other things,
Visions we're supposed to see.

A woman screams,
"Tune!"
Mouth from ear to ear.
Fingers dancin' Braille.
She's amazin',
So amazin',
Wonderful.

Oh come on,
Of course she's wonderful,
She's just fell in love with a tune.

We're a spin of the soul,
Turn of the age,
The centrifugal
A force.
Middle-aged hearts run free,
Free and connected to the need.
Tonight I'm needin' freein' with people I love,
Don't wanna know their names.
I'm freakin' with people I love
And I know they love me.
I'm needy,
Freaky,
And they love me.

So much of this is the sea.
And with my hands in the air,
Hips in Salsa,
I'm tuned into this archipelago
And not turnin' back the tide.

No words
And their mouths keep movin',
Can't stop tellin' joy.
Conversation's in mirror-ball.
Full stops,
Dance steps,
Neon dashes a nightscape.

I'm lit Morse code
Dot dot dance.
Tonight I'm dancin' with fallin' in love.
Dot dot dance
Dot dot dance

Dot dot dance.

And there you are.

Vision.

For the first,
Last
And everything.
A chat up line two seconds away from forever.

Arms drape wet velvet weight.
I sink and stand.
I'm damp with you,
Stink of you.

You sing *The Promise*.
I believe every word.
Were fallin' in love,
Burstin' joy.
We are these drugs,
This booze,
The win,
The lose,
The room
Its museum.
Its only exhibit.
It's rhythm 'n' blues,
Doin' our do
In ruby shoes.

In a glass cage with you
Fallin',
Callin'.
You're like blood,
Oxygen and thought.
History and thought.

You sing
And I say yes to
The promise you made.
I remember
The promise you made.
Pretty sure I'm the promise you made.

I own the world tonight.
I own my life.
I own you tonight,
Part of belonging.
You own me tonight,
Never let me go.
We are both sixteen tonight,
Your cheek rests on mine.
I believe in God tonight,
You wrap me in your wings.
I will teach you to fly tonight
If you'll bring me in to land.

Thirty-six hours tonight,
Thirty-six hours,
We're thirty-six hours old
And I have never felt so complete and in love.

And you are beautiful.
Perfection
Inside and out.
You're here resting on my shoulder
And somewhere else in time.
I know you like nostalgia
Like Sangria.
Carry you like St Christopher,
Like air.
My words can't pin you down

I'll never let love ruin this love,

I promise.
Beautiful like night,
Like lies,
Like solitude.
Solitude,
Like the promise you made.
Misty,
Like the promise you made.

Tonight I'm dancin' with fallin' in love.
Tonight I'm dancin with you.
Tonight I'm dancin' with lies
And I'm fallin' in love
With you.

My dreams tell me the story
Of another dance.
Oh come on,
That's the promise you made.

"*The Promise*.
Tune!"

A Trilogy Of Vole

Not long after that wild and furious incident, and starting to play with sobriety, I met and fell immediately in proper love with Shaun. We met where waterfalls whisper secrets. After eight years of being single, I got caught, hook, line and sinker. The poems from here to Superb *are a poetic diary of our funny old journey together. An inner-city tower block journey of love.*

1. Jaunty Angle

Wears himself at a jaunty angle,
Stylish, carefree.
Sports a shining spangle
And repartee eclectic,
Dizzying,
Electric.
Phrases spilling, gem-like,
Waterfalling colours,
Midsummer dreamings.
Puck,
Quixotic for a dreary millennium.

Deliriums of language and images.
He'd have been drowned as a warlock
By villagers with pitchforks,
Lit tawny from flaming torches
In the old days.

There's magic,
A somewhere else-ness.
I think he dreams awake.

Walks himself at a jaunty angle,
A tad Madchester about the knees.
Mystery rounds the eyes.
He could tell you anything, winking

With one eye visible from under that broad brim.
So completely him.
Makes me howl.
Werewolves breathing laughing gas,
Just us, and the moon, hysterical.
There's a path leading somewhere,
A whatever of who knows where or what,
And pastimes of adventuring in his words
And giggles.

There's truth,
Grounded wisdom.
I believe he could turn mud into lager.

2. Wrapped

We're in it,
Wrapped.
Tangled.
Alphabetti Spaghetti spelling out 'together',
Ribboned in language and intention.
Gifts chosen without picking.
Wrapping paper people
Cut by round-ended scissors,
A hand in hand garland
Who all encompass and map out the rough spots.

Gift
Wrapped
In me,
Me in him.
Taught and tender.
Skin stretched to blanket bends of imagination,
Cats cradling emotion.
There's a shelf of him for every finger,
Thigh,

Nook and cranky of me.
There's a lamppost of me for every
Lean he dreams and nightmare he fights.
Wanna be his hero, shooting the bad guys.
Wanna be the melody of his lullaby.

Cried one night when he was sleeping.
Proud, embarrassed,
Wanted him to see.
Didn't want him to see.
It's a conundrum when you're wrapped.

Him in me,
A presence.
A charge dissolving reality.
Gift.
I feel the rap of joy,
The gift of pain.
A present,
Present,
Resonates
In the infinites of flesh.

Never felt more alive.
Died twice last night,
Was resurrected for a third time.
Le Grand Mort,
A lot of life.
A lot of stuff.

We thought fight,
Mind hug,
Dress buff,
Heart thug,
Third sight.
Smile at the same time
And recognise the anagram on the quiz show:

VOLE.

I'm burrowing in.
The us of us,
The him of him,
The me of me,
The we of this.
The rant of me,
The question of him,
The gift of us,
The niggle.
Jiggles in the disco,
Giggles in the duvet,
Drinking in the bar,
Shouting down the phone.
Weeping alone,
Lying on the couch,
In bed,
In sleep.
Me and my fellah,
Wrapped.

3. Jaunty Angel

Back streets and alleys
Are heaven and home to someone.
Heaven and home.
A wanderer's address,
Seafarer's mission,
A ponderer's mansion housing the twisted ankle
Of romance.
The jaunty angle of jaundiced and jollied
Experience.

Heaven and hell,
Home to some tear-sodden dream.

This dreamer laments his history without you,
His torments,
Triumphs,
Ripped up tickets of
Theatre for two,
Wishes you were his companion when
He played Doctor Who.
Mind set firmly on the future.

Time machine entrenched
In the haven and always of yester-years.
A back-street dreamer,
Head made of stars,
His head's his favourite bars.
Doesn't matter to him women are from Venus,
Men from Mars.
Thinks you're alien enough to have crafted the universe,
Human enough
To make it work.

There there,
Now now
And then then.
Loves the near near,
The where where
And the
There you are of this.
This traveller wants you to share his journey,
Sightsee his tough places,
Rough guide his tenderness,
Map out his senses.
Be the magical mystery
He's wished away countless voyages to discover.

You're a northern star
Shining majestically in Aladdin's Cave,
The pound shop he loved in the undiscovered county

Of Scottie Road.
A Sacred Heart mirror flipping into hyperspace,
Chocolate coins with the king's face,
A prince inside a toad,
Bubble bath for ninety-nine pence,
'Heaven Scent' (that religious perfume
For Aunty Esther's Christmas Box),
Soap on a Rope,
Nope,
Pope on a Rope,
Socks,
Myrrh, frankincense,
A January sale surprise,
A triumphant loser scouring the skies,
Ice cream Sundays,
A tender bruiser,
The colours he always wanted his eyes,
A back-street boozer on his way to Oz.

You're mint,
You're safe,
You're top,
You're boss.

This time traveller's paddling,
Puddled in the sea on the Planet of Vole
With a spare bucket and spade.

Pop-O-Matic Love

Takes centre stage,
Jumping-Jacks across it.
Hip-hops,
Flick-flacks,
Higgledy-piggaldy
Gymnast physicality.
Slip-slops,
Can't direct it.
Doesn't take direction.
Upstages like camp characters in soaps.
Bunny-hops,
Flip-flops.
Hopes.

Tuppa, tuppa, tuppa.
Pop-O-Matic dice
Popping in a plastic dome.
Tuppa, tuppa, tuppa.
Frrrrrrustration!
Headache!
Crash bang wallop,
Boom bang-a-bang,
Tuppa, tuppa, tuppa.
Pop-O-Matic boom,
Pop-O-Matic bang.
Pop-O-Matic love
Has you questioning
What's right.
The dice.
Answers are a meaningless
That shine bright after an argument.
You'll argue again and both be right and wrong.

Love,

A kick in the balls.
A hangover.
Dirty smalls.
Red sock in a white noise
And the endless dry-cleaning of promises.

Love sucks like a problematic crack whore,
Toothless, raw;
Sticks jagged like an automatic door,
Locks like a geriatric jaw
Round an ever decreasing everlasting gobstopper.
An agoraphobic space hopper.
An exquisite marble mosaic ignored on a disco'd dancefloor.
Love is less and love is
'More More More
How d'ya like it
How d'ya like it?'

Who would we be without crippling feelings of jealousy,
The running on empty,
Hollowed out stomach,
And the heartbreak of a missed call?

Tuppa, tuppa, tuppa.
There must be something more fulfilling
Than feeling inadequate.
Oh you can't direct it,
Love's in control
Of being out of control.
Tuppa, tuppa, tuppa.
Pop-O-Matic,
Pop-O-Matic,
Leading the way of all directions,
A here, there and an everywhere.
Tuppa, tuppa, tuppa.
Like a dog with six noses
In a mansion full of shit,

A bipolar condition without diagnosis,
A cheeky faced urchin waiting to be hit.
Bloody nosed and
Three sixes.

But when you breathe it,
Slowly take it in,
Really breathe it
(And you have to honestly breathe),
Its scent invigorates
Like snorting life.
Real life,
Like no other life before.
Barnstorms like a herd,
Buffalos your mind,
Dust storms,
Thunderclaps applause.
Earth after a thunderstorm.
Heaven after Earth.

Because when you breathe him,
Baby, you're really breathing.
Lungs balloon planet-size.
The hungry eat,
Water's free,
And the answer to everything
Is just you two.
Tuppa, tuppa, tuppa.

Love so completely Pop-O-Matics
Old romantics.
Tantrics,
Teaches dogs new tricks,
Lays the law.
Washing billowing on a line
Semaphores.
It's the just,

In the nick of time.
A line of coke.
Addiction,
Affliction,
A joke.

That bloke in a mood
Who chokes you up with feeling,
Really chokes you up with feeling,
Until you can feel no more.
Then you feel more.

'More More More
How d'ya like it
How d'ya like it?'

And alone's a distant cousin you've forgotten the name of.
A battlefield of roses
As pinpoint accurate as the word juxtaposes.

Oh it's war,
A *phwooaarrr,*
Tuppa, tuppa, tuppa,
But one well worth fighting for.

Mmmmm . . . *tuppa, tuppa, tuppa.*
Crazy in love.
Mmmmm . . . Pop-O-Matic crazy in love.

Don't Be A Dickhead, Gerry

Sobriety is an odd elusive beast, one that sometimes slips its leash. Being drunk can be the best thing ever, but sometimes . . . Meff is a Scouse word for idiot.

You can be a dickhead, Gerry.
Tool!
You fall out your life, charging head first,
Taking chances with chances,
Chasing foolhardy notions of blurred absolutism.
Drunken absolutism.
Worst kind.

You can be a dickhead, Gerry.
You don't know everything.
Yes, even you,
Fool!
You endanger the cocoon of love,
Split it open.
Splat!
A bust lip
Drips
Insipid droplets of blood,
Staining polka dot crimson
The shine-white floor of security,
And, if you joined the dots,
It would read in bright red spidery scribble,
Meff!

What makes you think things so wrong could be so right?
Sometimes, Gerry, you make my toes curl;
Mutant Quavers,
Take my breath away
And take the biscuit.

Crumbs!

It's a wonder you're still alive.
You deserved that smack.
Crack!
Such a knobhead, Gerry,
With your hobnob bluff and bluster,
With your Sergeant Major Shout Shout
And machismo.
Go take your head for a rest.
Deserved.
Shower it in the fragrant pitter-pat
Of rose petals.
Hover.
Tell it to white feather on the tail winds of whispers,
Murmur the gentle of summer breezes.

Give your abandonment issues a breather,
Leave them alone,
Let them wander.
Let them window shop.
Help them buy a new direction,
Give them a spring in their step.
Boing!
And send them merrily on their way.

Shine, Gerry.
Wings.
Be that Booby Dazzler,
Gleam!
Flash Roger Moore teeth
And mosey through life,
Alert and alive.
Alive!
Don't be a cliché, Gerry,
Don't gay out,
Don't be an idiot.
Don't!
Too clever to be that stupid.

Dickhead!

The Memory Shop

A simple journey after some difficult news.

It was on the street
Opposite the hospital
Shaun said something about computers.
I didn't understand,
It was digital retro-babble
Set in the future.
Something about memory sticks
And time.

I called it The Memory Shop.
It looked like a shop.
Old,
Red brick.
A shop that bought and sold
Memory.
What was it again?
Ah yes,
The Memory Shop.
A shop.
A pawn shop,
Three baubles are a memory
Lending time.

Dusty as the tops of shelves.
Maybe it was
The porn shop.
A guilty room,
Unthought through
Violence.
Screams are loud
And they're paid for.

I'm for sale.
Little plastic figures,
Double-jointed
And manoeuvrable.
Seven of me
With eagle eyes.
Squeeze the back of my heads
And watch me watch,
Pull my strings
And I'll say the same things forever.
Some will say automaton,
Some will say poet.
I'm in the bargain bin,
Vulnerable,
Hoping one day I'll be collectable,
Able to say things
To the future.

My family and friends,
Chipped whimsies
Animated by wishing,
Guffawing
And incomplete.

I'm there between the pages of
Annuals
And Bibles,
Dennis the Menace
And Jesus Christ.
I was crucified by lies
And 'the slipper'.
I liked being pesky.

All for sale,
Making offers
We can't refuse.
Sometimes you can't believe in things

When you need to survive.

Shaun carried on about computers.
I didn't understand.
I want to buy time from The Memory Shop
So we can last forever.

Memory sticks.
We're all antiques.

Shaun's On The Moon

Rocket ships and galaxies,
Nebulae and fantasies,
Shaun's on the Moon.
Daydreams and dance steps.
Sing-songs on door steps,
Shaun's on the Moon.

Shaun's on the Moon,
Up in the air
Teaching moonbeams to
Michael Jackson and Fred Astaire.
He's doing this without any air.
Shaun's on the Moon.

Shaun's on the Moon,
Ever so French,
Sat ooh la la
On a star-studded bench
Learning aliens to talk posh,
À la Dame Judi Dench.
Shaun's on the Moon.

'Chanson D'Amour'.

Shaun's on the Moon
Conducting tides,
Forming continents,
Oceans wide.
He's doing this
Even though he's tired.
Oh yes, Shaun's on the Moon.

Shaun's on the Moon,
A high-kicking Jarvis Cocker

Singing the odd Richard Ashcroft cover.
Even learnt to
Strictly flamenco and hover.
Shaun's on the Moon.

Shaun's on the Moon,
Free as a bird.
All the good things he's ever heard,
All the care he's ever cared,
Fruity zest of lemon curd.

Shaun's on the Moon,
Sat with Doctor Who
Discussing K9 and Sarah Jane, too.
Asks,
"Doctor,
Just who Who is Who?"
Shaun's on the Moon.

Shaun's on the Moon
With a wee dram of sherry.
My man in the Moon,
A little merry,
Looking at the Earth,
A tiny blueberry.
Shaun's on the Moon.

Shaun's on the Moon
Writing a letter to Mars.
On the Moon
Reconfiguring stars.

Hungry

A walk in the snow
To an appointment.
Choppy,
Axe murderer in an ice-bucket,
Molotov cocktail on the rocks.
Our feet,
Comedy feet,
Slipping.
Never quite falling over.

Conversation muffled as tramping.
Everyone hugging against the cold.
Snowsialism.

And I look at him,
He's dancing on the ice
Like he dances in my head,
Quirky and adorable.
I talk to him.
Listen.
We're hungry.

You

Out in the up and up,
Posturing for luck.
I beg the Seven Seas for their lot.
Treasure trove.

Gift me sound,
Splendour me words
And let rains drench me impossible.

A word in your shell-like salty lips.

Got glory in my hands
And in the way they move,
Ghosts in my feet
And in the way they groove.

And I want to tell you you're wonderful,
That the shine of heart is diamond on you.
And I want to tell you your history,
That you ride time innocently and nobly.

Picture me imperfect summer,
Mirror me in dew
And we'll toss aside associations of grim.

I see you tall with grandmothers
And their tales of apple pie.

Superb

Life huh!
The way it so often twists 'n' turns,
Fire of a sun before it burns;
Untaught, before they learn.
Superb!

Spinning of a sixpence,
Dizzying behind the whirl of a sports car.
Distance near yet so far,
Time light takes to travel from a star.
Superb!

Telling stories of past life recession,
Conquering overwhelming weights of depression.
Some things are tender in the arms of obsession.
Superb!

I once met a man who shone like light.
I asked for advice.
"Don't let me tell you what to do," he said.
I said, "Please don't tell me that. I'll do what I tell me to do,
But, hopefully, I'll be able to take some advice from you.
You've lived long, seven hundred years to be precise.
Used and been used.
Stop trying to be so underwhelmingly Zen."
Mr Light looked somewhat confused.
Superb!

Superb!
The shine off chip fat,
The there and whyfores informing this and that,
Heads angled under jaunty hats.
Welcome made poetry on grubby mats.

Superb!
Shivers made pleasure dancing off your spine,
The ability to disable the uselessness of 'Mine!'
Knowing everything could eventually rhyme.
Dinner time.

Superb!
Those wartime stories of my Grandmother,
The Grand Guignol darkness of my older brother,
Relishing the genius of other.
Why bother.

I used to visit a ghost who refused to scare.
She said, "It's not so much the scaring, Gerry,
Scaring's a piece of piss. It's the consequences.
I'm frightened of the consequences."
Superb!

Middle-Aged Spread

Episode I: An Adventure In Time And Pace

There's this kid, can't be more than ten, sees himself as a bit of a story teller. Tells stories to his mum, send-to-sleep stories. It's not bedtime yet. His mum's watching the telly, her mid-evening soap, Emmerdale Farm. She's so engrossed that the kid can only see her bum and the varicosed tangle of American tanned legs. He likes this, a favourite angle: cosy, familiar and funny. The smell of hot margerined toast is fading; still has half a mug of too-sweet tea.

The warm of the log-effect gas fire illuminates; he is the happy victim of its autumnal strobing. He cuddles himself into the folds of an old faux leather armchair, part of a three piece suite. Bits of it are peeling. This particular chair has been handed down through generations. His brother Paul owned it before him, brother Chris before him. It's been in the family for at least four years. He picks at it and it peels like sunburned skin.

For this kid, the chair is not a place to be bored, watching his mum's Rubenesque arse and choice of programme. This chair is his kingdom and he is the king of imagination. The chair is playtime. It was a galleon yesterday, a stagecoach the day before. Today it'll be a spaceship, no, not a spaceship, a space-chair. A space-chair that can travel anywhere, from the furthest star all the way to the corner shop, even the past and future.

He's excited and secretive, not even his mother's bottom must know.

In his head, the humming of engines. He's comforted by the confidence of secrets and the promise of time travel, it's all part of the vibration. Everything clicks into gear, leather becomes metal. The arms of the chair twist, turning into holo-dimensional control panels. The erratic sounds of beeping ping-pong precariously, pitter-pattering a neon pulse. He's ready. The dome initialises the final stages of closing. He sets the thrusters on stand-by. There's a big red shiny button. There's always a big red shiny button, even in the galleon, even in the stagecoach.

Presses the big red shiny button.

Sinks back, resigned to the pressure of taking off. His face stretches and blurs. His elfin features made absurd by the comedy of gravity. The chair slowly rises. Stops, then ZAP! Jets invincible and imaginary into the gaudy splendour of a sprawling inviting hyperspace.

There's nothing to suggest he was even there, except the billowing of pink net curtains and a slight smell of scorching.

*

One day you're born. You've no idea how many days you'll have. Being born and there you are, just there. No thoughts of much, most definitely no thoughts of middle age. Just needing and being. Being born means you're perpetually in the middle. In the middle of immortality. In the middle of arguments you've inadvertently caused. In the middle of your family and the big wide world, both a blessing and nuisance.

Maybe that's what we stay, a blessing and nuisance let loose on a world of blessings and nuisances. I've come to terms with my own destiny to be both these things. Sometimes I've been a blessing and nuisance in disguise. I've blessed nuisances with my advice. I've cursed nuisances with my advice. I've been a nuisance cursed and blessed by my own and others advice. There's no end to the blessings and curses, it seems.

No sooner has being born happened than you start to crawl on a primordial carpet of tea stains and fag ash. Into the middle of the living room floor, encouraged by your family to eventually walk, from all fours to your knees then upright on your legs. "C'mon, Gerard, that's it, one foot in front of the other . . . C'mon, Gerard, c'mon." Evolving your way to a table leg or arm of a chair. It's all about limbs, names and arms of chairs, that stage of life. And there you are, being cajoled and overjoyed to be coerced into becoming a man. A bubbling bundle of pink nonsense with ideas above your station. No sooner do they teach you to talk, they tell you to shut up. Bliss. If only life could remain so silly.

"C'mon, Gerard!"

When do things stop being simple? Maybe that toddle across the living room carpet isn't as easy as it's cabbage-looking. Maybe that toddle across the living room carpet is the most complicated thing we ever do. It's all relative after all. Or is it all relatives? I for one would love that to be the single most difficult thing I've done.

"C'mon, Gerard. One foot in front of the other!"

Funny, that being born thing. One of the great things about being born is the imponderability of it all.

When do we first ask questions?

When are those questions relevant?

Are questions the wobbly of learning to walk?

"C'mon, Gerard!"

When do we stop learning?

Being born.

Bah!

At eighteen I thought middle age would be the time I knew it all. Now middle-aged, I think the eighteen year old me knew a lot more. He was a frightened effervescent chap, vulgar and subtle, inquisitive to distraction and gloriously impervious to answers. A camp flourish and a well rehearsed smile were all he needed to deal with the world. I'm selling him a little short. A camp flourish, a well rehearsed smile and a new Soft Cell album were all he needed to deal with the world. He was kind and stupid and thought he was clever.

At eighteen, still in the middle, stumbling aloof like a glamorous toddler. Trying out dances. Such dances. Sharp and distancing, underconfident and chic. Trying to find a dance that makes you look cool and not that knob in the middle of the club.

What is rhythm?

Trying out the elegant walk from the dance floor back to your drink.

Still in the middle, trying to please others around us.

When do we stop dancing?

When do eyes stop judging and do we ever dance for ourselves?

I know I've danced for myself.

When, then, have I danced for others?

How is it I know I've danced for myself?

Did we do the twist?

I'm not trying to lose people in the vortex of possibilities, just fascinated at the pin-point moment when all this happens. As much as I love the imponderability of it all, it can also piss me off.

That eighteen year old can piss me off, but, boy, do I still love the imponderability of him all.

Here I am, middle-aged, and stuck in the middle of my own middle. Twisted, in a dodgems and fairy lights kind of way. I have little advice, but I do have experiences. I think they're really good, experiences. A blessing and a curse. Nuisances.

Glad I've had and have them.

Glad I've had and have fairy lights.

*

Zooming into planetary orbit in his space-chair, the Story Teller bounces off the outer film of the atmosphere, skimming like a pebble on a lake. Monitors have shown the Earth has spun disastrously off its psychotronic axis, that it's emotional and physical integrity is in danger of fracturing. To recalibrate its emotive-matter matrix would take an enormous surge of electromagnetic psychotronic energy. Psychotronic energy of that clarity and definition can only be found in the imagination of a child and the engine of a space-chair.

The Story Teller knows the only way to save the earth is to sacrifice the space-chair, but if he does that then he condemns himself to the lifestyle of an Earth-Man. He's visited planet Earth long enough to know that Earth-Men have the ridiculous propensity to resign themselves to too few choices. He even knows an Earth-Man who delights in working for the same company for the rest of his life. This same Earth-Man rejoices in the knowledge that some Earth-Men are unemployed and roars with laughter at some of them being unemployable.

What does the Story Teller do? Does he start the chain-reaction of psychotronic ultra-waves that reduces him and his space-chair to dust? Or does he save the Earth and end up with a job?

There are precious few seconds left.

Does the Story Teller choose oblivion or the inconsistency of democracy?

Middle-Aged Spread

Episode II: An Adventure In Time And Face

The Story Teller presses the big red shiny button on his ever-glowing control panel of colours and beeps.

KIIIIIZERRRKKKTT!!!!!!!

A concertina-like judder leaves him momentarily out of phase. He is neon breadcrumbs twisting furiously in a hypersticial blender. Finally, he catches up with himself and becomes neon bread. The big red shiny button has created a stasis field around the Earth. The stasis has the desired effect: time is frozen, giving him precious minutes to think. Although it doesn't solve anything, it stops the Earth and the space-chair cracking to cinders. The Story Teller feels at once calm, jittery, doughy and well lit.

Perhaps he should let the Earth dissolve into the mindless heap of broken biscuits it's become and find contentment on another planet in another time . . . Perhaps not.

He has friends, family and a life about to unfold on that planet.

Perhaps he cannot.

*

"C'mon, Gerard!"

The performer is a strange beast indeed. Jangling and whispering, quite often singing and shouting. Just what is the performer about? As a performer, I'm intrigued by my need *to be*. People sometimes make the mistake that the performer is a courageous confident being, striding like a colossus over the failings of humanity . . . Often that's what they mistake poets for.

As a performance poet, my audience is inclined to think I know what's right. I don't wish to disappoint. I only kind of know what might be right for me. Not being selfish or selfless here, but that's about it really. I'm a lucky performer because a large part of my audience wants what I want.

I believe the performer has to be artistically wrong as well as right to make the performance work. What I mean is that 'right' is wrong. That's why religion can never work, because it labours under the auspice that it's always right, that it knows the truth. That it knows the truth and is always right. Always right, knows the truth – oh, and you are wrong and a liar and it is right and knows the truth. Religion: the longest running farce in history and it looks set to run on and on.

The performer must be flawed and, like any great clown, be able to topple ingloriously into the idiocy of his own ramblings. In many ways the performer is the ultimate victim, seemingly and powerfully in control, but at risk as snowflakes in a heat-wave. Look at Piaf, Garland or Bassey: snowflakes with big voices on their way to Honolulu.

The performer needs to be vulnerable, it's his life's work. No-one loves a smart-arse. Unless it's a smart-arse like Lenny Bruce, who, in no particular order, was a genius, smackhead and snowflake.

Our world has been shaped by genius smackheads, by snowflakes.

Just like religion, the performer needs to be right about being wrong to survive.

I love performing.

It's in me, real as electromagnetic psychotronic energy. I can't imagine my life without it and, like all performers, my need to perform is greater than my material. The world needs performers. It needs to see wobbly inconsistent superhero versions of itself. By that, I mean the time-shattering talent of Jacques Brel and the shabby kick-about nonsense of The Krankies, both as perversely valid as each other. For me, art can't be about nodding and murmuring. It has to be about unveiling, and no-one unveils the human condition quite like Jacques Brel and The Krankies. The best things I see are the things that bring me closer to myself and us closer to us.

I've been a performer one way or another since I was sixteen. Now middle-aged, I see the fragility of it more. After years of trying to make the world a better place and watching it nose-dive into its own capitalist Armageddon, you'd think I'd know better. Why don't I just get a job or marry an accountant? One of the great sadnesses of being a middle-aged performer is coming to terms with never really changing the world.

The only thing I've done outside of performing is bartending in one of gay Manchester's most infamous bars, New York New York. I was forty-six. I worked there for six months.

Being a barman simply means you are the director of a piece of theatre that can never be shown to the paying public because it's the paying public who are its stars. Being a barman cemented my thought: everything is performance, life's a blizzard, we are all snowflakes and soon it'll be summer. We're born, we toddle across the living room floor, we try and change the world, and eventually end up buying cheap vodka and coke in New York New York. Or we become stand up priests, sermonising comics or smackheads. Or, if we're really lucky, end up as doctors, or married. Or, if the stars are perfectly aligned, maybe married to a heroin-addicted doctor who dabbles in a little bit of stand-up.

Phew!

The only difference between a performer and a drunk is that a performer will one day act being a drunk and then get drunk after the show.

Perhaps we need performers like we need drink.

The performer, always in the middle of tormented juxtaposition.

Perhaps we need performers like we need drink.

*

From the inner reaches of outer space, the Story Teller hovers. Three seconds to make a decision. Amazing how long seconds can last, he thinks. Not knowing what will happen, he releases the big red shiny button.

SSSKKKREEEEEEEAAALLLAAATTTEZZZIIIZZZICZZICZZIC!

There is an overwhelming feel of somethings. Becomes all the colours he's ever imagined, tastes of purple and orange. He is vibrating from physicality into shadow. Such neon shadows. There is more than sound, more than vision. Isomorphic inversion deafens. He is being pulled. Every stretch of his skin alive with energy. He has never felt such terrifying bliss. He wonders with joy: Is this death?

Then the amoral veil of blackness.

The Story Teller wakes into a semi-mumbled laugh, feels drunk. Half of his face is damp with dew, rich and sticky. He is lying in thick luscious grass. How has this happened, he wonders, and what is that heat? Wave after wave of extraordinary warmth, beating down on him like a giant's breath . . . He breathes with them. Refuses to move, enjoys the overwhelming calm of their weight. There are sounds whirling above, high-pitched and hypnotic, perhaps the callings of exotic birds. The white shimmer before he opens his eyes is intense with sun. Opens his eyes, sun-blind. Takes time to focus. His world blurs slowly into reality, then super-fast impossibility.

In front of him, a pink, red, fleshy chasm. The stench of rotten meat, hanging limp like dead bodies on rows of sharpened tombstones. A roar from the heart of Satan. He is tiny, looks up to face the open slavering jaw of a Tyrannosaurus Rex.

Middle-Aged Spread

Episode III: An Adventure In Time And Grace

Fear had never felt so horrifically terrifying. The Story Teller's immediate response was to run, run as fast as his jellied legs could carry him. Then just in the nick . . . something clicked, that bit of knowledge that won't be bullied by fear. That knowledge was a voice. A voice like no other, gentle and assertive, disembodied and real. It simply said, "C'mon Gerard." The Story Teller knew immediately to freeze, be still as the stillest statue.

He'd heard the voice before; sometimes when in great crisis, sometimes at anytime. It only ever said "C'mon, Gerard." He trusted it and froze, didn't even move his eyes. The Tyrannosaurus looked puzzled; had its prey disappeared? Its enormous neck wound a slow, determined, ninety degree angle around the lavish vista. The Story Teller remained stuck, oblivious to its arching elegance.

High above he heard a squawk, no longer the sound of exotic birds; it was cawing, wretched. Even though he couldn't look, he guessed it must be a Pterodactyl. Instinctively, he knew he was hearing his only chance of survival. Distracted, the Tyrannosaurus jerked violently away from the Story Teller, and, sensing its new prey, hurled itself upward. With an incredible reach and stretch of its body, it leaped and snapped up the Pterodactyl in the bite of a second. Crunch of bone and flesh echoed as the ground trampolined wildly under the weight of its landing, shaking the forest with an earthquake.

After wringing the Pterodactyl to its final neck-breaking end, the Tyrannosaurus peered around one last time. The Story Teller could taste his heart and the sweat off his forehead. Then, looking like it had forgotten something mildly important, the great beast marched effortlessly and cockily away.

*

My grandmother lives in my spirit. She is a constantly informing sensibility. She died when I was about ten, a slight woman with a thin, authoritative, voice. I remember a real coal fire always raging in her bottom floor flat, her ability to feed you without moving a muscle, and trilling of stories. She seemed ancient to me and I couldn't always hear what she was saying. I loved her being in total denial of her deafness. I would often sit in the same room just soaking her in. I knew I was in the presence of a very special entity. My grandmother was kind. Profoundly kind. An understanding woman, who wouldn't suffer unfairness in anyone, and you became automatically kinder in her company. Whatever gentle magic she embodied, it spilt into you. Even living in the all white area of Scotland Road of the '20s and '30s, she wouldn't tolerate anyone being racist and would stop them mid-sentence. Without ever declaring herself a socialist, she was the most socialist person I had, and have ever, known.

In the beginning of the Second World War my grandma owned a simple grocery shop. As the war took its toll rations became short. Quite often, desperate mothers would send their children with little hand-written notes to her shop. The notes would read something like, "Mary, we are starving, could you please give us some bread on tick?"

Some of the notes didn't even have writing, just a series of scribbles; thankfully my grandma could read scribble. It was always bread they asked for. Bread in Scottie Road is as biblical as Moses. My grandma would always give away the bread and whatever else she had in the shop, so much so she eventually lost the business. My mother told me my grandma knew the kids may be lying, but she would still give away her stock. She did that because she never knew if they were truly lying, and would rather starve herself than knowingly see a child without bread.

In these days of unrelenting greed and mindless acquisition, this story feeds me. Even though she knew she was being ripped-off, my grandmother could not cope with the thought of a child without bread. Of course, the end of the business brought her own family toppling into crippling poverty. My mother would tell me that even though they had nothing in the cupboards my grandma would somehow find something for them to eat.

Mary Prescott had knowledge. It was a knowledge born of a simple credo, a credo that now is laughed at and reduced to scorn: sharing.

And sharing wasn't easy, sometimes it was difficult and caused great hardship, but Mary Prescott knew the true value of it. She was as valid as a breath and stoic as an oak. The respect my grandma had from her family and community was so tangible you could rearrange the letters and re-spell it, and it would still read respect. The stories born of and around her bind and colour my art.

Sometimes, when I'm out and about, I do genuinely hear my name being called. It's disembodied and ethereal and can happen when there isn't a soul around. I'm an atheist, so I don't believe in ghosts or gods. It's obviously an aural hallucination and one I am totally comfortable with. It brings me great joy when I hear it and connectivity to the best bits of my childhood. Not only my childhood, but to the history of understanding and giving, implicit in its timbre. It's heavy with kindness, commands immense respect and love. It's a woman's voice, thin and authoritative.

"C'mon, Gerard."

*

The Story Teller decides to leave the pre-history of his imaginings with a song in his heart. Meandering back to the space-chair, his thoughts are a mishmash of melody fusing. He realised long ago he had a big head for a kid, the size of a football pitch and a poem. His journey back to the space-chair had him inspired by the thrill of adventuring. He promised himself, there and then, he was going to have many more and would delight in documenting them. He felt the insides of stories and experience. It's almost as if they were the same thing.

The once treacherous jungle now seems benign and still, a gentle backdrop to his blissed-out mood. He could, if he wanted, turn this moment into a horrific cliff-hanger, full of danger and emotional turmoil, but decides against it. Instead, he'll end this instalment relaxed and pondering.

He replicates a bottle of dandelion and burdock, boiled ham and tomato sandwiches, a packet of smoky bacon crisps and a Topic. Maybe he'll see off 'The Aliens of Terror' a bit later on. He's content now, relaxing into the soft faux-leather of the space-chair. Marc Bolan sings Twentieth Century Boy *while his eye-lids pitter-pat sleep. Thoughts of games and Emma Peel fade to dreams. The Story Teller's mouth smiles limply as he assuredly drops off.*

David

This is about my very dear friend, David Hoyle. David has been an artist and performer for many years. He has held audiences captivated and outraged. There has never been, or will be, an artist like him. I feel like I've known him for a kind of forever and suddenly, after forever, here we are both middle-aged and both still hoofin' a tap-dance for the world. For you, my friend.

Has there ever been energy
So trailblazing?
Essential as breath,
Unquenchionable as youth,
Effortless as Bette Davis smoke?
Magnificent queen,
Elegant dragon,
Breathing hot
And out;
A world-weary effervescence
Ready to burn.
Burn babies burn.
Fire talkin',
Smokin'!
Has there ever been such bravery?

Words direct as arrows.
Has there ever been such archery?

Cheek leaving you spell-bound.
Has there ever been such saucery?

Genderless Phoenix,
Paint-splattered Minnelli and Guevara.
Elvis Garland
Spending rock 'n' roll suicide at
Heart-Break motel
With the men who got away.

Made up by spit-fire,
Shot down by life,
Psyche-strewn and
Bludgeoned,
Messy as an artist's pallet.
If there's Bassey to be had
Then let's have it.
Has there ever been a more decorative
Survivor?
Has there?
Champagne!
Campaign!
Cocaine!

Has there ever been such laughter?
Tears of the profound and profane.
Ever doubted what you're seeing?
What you are actually seeing.

If you can't bear the truth
He'll bare it for you.
Bare all,
Bar none.
Being.

Stories scarred as jealousy,
Teeth able to rip
The macabre from society.
Dead meat.
Every sinew, every vein
Ready to wrap mediocrity.
Kebab.
Humanity is eating itself.
Melody.
A mirror of flesh and bone.
Orchid.
Vaudeville monster.

My avant guardian angel.
I know only the hurt are allowed this sight.

One night
I saw you explode.
Spread over the road,
A Sacred Heart attack on Vauxhall,
Animated by accidents
And ancients.
A display of pizzazz and insecurity,
Earth-quaking artistry,
The D
Of the Big Bang,
Big Bang fairy.
A stand-up comet,
Meteor-fall on cabaret.
The shakes of reality,
The easy explosion of how it could be,
Flesh torn,
Release of humanity.
Beauty.
A soul,
Stretching.
A child bearing pain.
The birth of honesty.

A deer on thin ice.
Languid as a stoned chaise longue.
Laugh like an ice pick
Hacking velvets of flesh.

Has there ever been energy
So ready for
The ache of the wounded,
The limp of the wrist,
For *now*.

Kebab.
Humanity.
Melody.
Orchid.

Encore!

Has there ever been energy
So intellectual and raw?

The Soldiering Of Soldiering On

There are always turning points. Life moments that rock you out of your sensibility and routine. Unfair on the surface and not necessarily about middle age. Respect to those moments and their teachings, both horrific and joyous.

This is not positivia.
I'm well aware a child somewhere
Is watching her mother die of AIDS,
That a trickle-down joy has made a smile.

A beach fire.
A scald.
A street party.

This is not a white-wash
Where we cleanse our chakras clarity blue.
It's simply the soldiering of soldiering on.
Because you have to,
Simply have to.

Unless you don't want to.
Can't.
That's a different story
And I understand it.

The wandering of wondering things,
The pond-life of pondering,
Because history isn't made up of ding-dong-dings.
That never happened.

This is water on a morning face,
Ting-a-ling-a-ling.
The mourning of a wintered state,
The demolition of fate,

Re-imagining of great.
It's a world, things happen.
It's the soldering of soldiering on.

This
Next breath I take,
Key I press,
Thought I hate,
Love,
Want,
It's filling time.
Stuff.
Nonsense.
It's the pressure of pressing on,
Because someone loves you.
Or will.
Or might.
Or can't.
Won't, even.
Not allowed.

Remember those amazing parties
Where laughter rediscovered humanity?

Because someone, somewhere, is making soup,
Brilliant soup.
Or crayoning a butterfly.
The lovely colours of crayons.

This is not positivia.
I'm well aware some people can't afford crayons
And we're training teenagers to shoot teenagers.
Simply the soldiering of soldiering on,
Because there's tea to drink
And monsters to manifest.
Toast.
Rages.

A stumble that makes you smile.
Those amazing parties.
There's a rhyme to hide in the miming of language.

Soup!
For God's sake man, there's soup,
Brilliant soup,
And we all know how that can taste.

It's ache.
It's kiss.
The murmuring of *Wuthering Heights*.
The jangle-woven danger of secrets.
The smell of a puppy.
Your first E.
That child's mother has died of AIDS.
Ting-a-ling-a-ling.
Snow.

It's A World, Things Happen

Here doggy doggy,
I got some good advice.
It's a world things happen!

Put that in your pipe and smoke it.
It's really good advice,
Means you do nowt about everything.
Means you've permission to shut down
Like rows of shops in eighty-four.
It's a trick, wisdom
That informs
And takes away.

Here doggy doggy,
I got some good advice.
It's straight hair, curls happen!

Make that damp sand in your bucket.
Let's call a spade a spade.
It's logic without reason
And drips like acid rain on a polystyrene city.

Oh come on, it's a polystyrene city, acid rain happens.

"In forty-five raindrops we're all going to die."

When sound bites
We listen.

Summits Or Nothings

Musings on a recurring dream. On a recurring life.

Head over six inch heels.
Killer.
Sooo over.
Got a dream height I just gotta conquer.
Gotta dance.
One inch away from the safety of the ledge,
Two hundred from the safety net.
I'm Gene Kelly,
Two miles from the routine.
Hair-raising.
Could just fall, I suppose.
So much falling,
Splattering my history.
Dream falling.
Never dreamt I fell.
Funny that.
Some stories just too tall to know.
Summits or nothings.
Someone once told me
You can learn how to listen.
I thank the pavement I'm self-taught.

Sometimes I Get Lost

I went to a funeral in November '09. Someone I've known for a very long time. It got me once again thinking about loss and about the loss that lives inside me. This is for Trevor and for the grief that lives in us all.

Put me in a balloon.
A brightly coloured balloon,
A balloon that tastes of biscuits.
The sweetest biscuits.
Pink wafers,
Light
And cloud-dunking,
Melt when you're dusking.
Gorgeous,
Gaudy,
Gaudi.

Point it at the sun.
Tell the sun to write a circus
And I'll be a clown.
A single-teared clown
That sobs when he's stumbling,
Cheery
When he's dumbing down,
Running around fool-heartedly
With a mouthful of confetti
And a bucket full of love.

And tell that balloon
It's not straight on till mourning,
That after the Moon and Jupiter
There's a party.
Such a party.
A party full of people
You can't invite to parties anymore.

Can you imagine the music,
The dancing?
Can you imagine the chatter?
A party you couldn't leave,
A party that tastes of rhythm and laughter,
Of happy ever after.
The party that never leaves us.
The party that bereaves us.

So, put me in a balloon,
Point me at that party.
I'll pin a tail on a donkey,
I'll blind man's bluff,
But let me take the blind-fold off
Because life's tough,
Rough and tumbling.
A buffoon bumbling.

Take me out this room,
Put me in that balloon,
Point me in the right direction
Because sometime I get loss.

Got Lost

In vacuous times my head succumbs
To a bullying of bashing itself.

Ever twatted yourself so hard
You wish you were someone else?
I have.
Do.

Could rip out my heart,
Splatter it against a wall
And watch the blood smear.
Coward.
Watch it fall into the gutter
And splutter, half-cock ,
Down a beaten track.

Cough
Cough.
Hack
Hack.

I could take out my intestines and hang myself,
Hear my spine crack,
Swing directionless from my yardarm.
Head-butt me with my shin,
Knock myself out with my thigh,
Break my chin.

Mind and body at war
With the soldiering
Of soldiering on.
And on
And on
And on

And on
And on.

The pointlessness.

The politeness.

The pity.

The parties.

It's hard to forgive yourself.

I'd like to laze
In summer
And haze a mizzle, too.
I'd like the days to become a
Busying of you.
I'd love our hearts to buttercup
An under the chin shine,
Love to etch the trees
With a
You will always be mine.
I want the river's babble to be
A gossiping of us.
I'd like bluebells in the skeleton
Of a red double-decker bus.

But sometimes I get lost.

Multiples And Lies

I've written about this before in Planet Young. *I just had to write about it again in* Planet Middle Age. *I once had a 'group' of friends I thought would be friends for the rest of my life. Some of these friends, in fact quite a lot of them, were middle-aged. They weren't kids . . . oh no no no, they were actually middle-aged, honest to God. We had a lot in common, it seemed. Some of them were even socialists. For a very inane and intangible reason they dumped me. Some of them had even been to university to get degrees. We, as a 'group', made the second summer of love last ten glorious comedic loving dancing years. Until it was swamped by the paranoid inconsistent individualist cocaine winter of malcontent. Some of them were vegetarians. I will never understand their cruelty. So far, they are the biggest disappointment of my middle age. I describe this poem as 'a fucked up rave ballad'. It's one of the saddest tomes I've ever written. Dedicated to, and my last memory of, 'The Group'.*

I'm in the beat of
I'm in the beat of
I'm in the beat of
Multiples and lies.
I'm in the beat of
I'm in the beat of
I'm in the beat of
Multiples and lies.
I'm in the beat of
I'm in the beat of
I'm in the beat of
Multiples and lies.
I'm in the beat of
I'm in the beat of
I'm in the beat of
Multiples and lies.
I'm in the beat of
I'm in the beat of
I'm in the beat of

Multiples and lies.
I'm in the beat of
I'm in the beat of
I'm in the beat of
Multiples and lies.

The dragon waits. He tucks a tear.
The dragon's waiting for the Devil to appear.
The dragon stands. The dragon breathes.
The dragon burns. The dragon seethes.

I'm in the beat of
I'm in the beat of
I'm in the beat of
Multiples and lies.
I'm in the beat of
I'm in the beat of
I'm in the beat of
Multiples and lies.
I'm in the beat of
I'm in the beat of
I'm in the beat of
Multiples and lies.
I'm in the beat of
I'm in the beat of
I'm in the beat of
Multiples and lies.
I'm in the beat of
I'm in the beat of
I'm in the beat of
Multiples and lies.
I'm in the beat of
I'm in the beat of
I'm in the beat of
Multiples and lies.

The dragon's offline. The dragon's offside.

The dragon means everything he says.
The dragon's gold mine. The dragon's mum died.
The dragon's dragging in a multiple of ways.

I'm in the beat of
I'm in the beat of
I'm in the beat of
Multiples and lies.
I'm in the beat of
I'm in the beat of
I'm in the beat of
Multiples and lies.
I'm in the beat of
I'm in the beat of
I'm in the beat of
Multiples and lies.
I'm in the beat of
I'm in the beat of
I'm in the beat of
Multiples and lies.
I'm in the beat of
I'm in the beat of
I'm in the beat of
Multiples and lies.
I'm in the beat of
I'm in the beat of
I'm in the beat of
Multiples and lies.

Swirly swirly. Swirly swirly. Swirly men cock beat and dive.
Swirly swirly. Swirly swirly. Swirly love resurrects and dies.

I'm in the beat of
I'm in the beat of
I'm in the beat of
Multiples and lies.
I'm in the beat of

I'm in the beat of
I'm in the beat of
Multiples and lies.
I'm in the beat of
I'm in the beat of
I'm in the beat of
Multiples and lies.
I'm in the beat of
I'm in the beat of
I'm in the beat of
Multiples and lies.
I'm in the beat of
I'm in the beat of
I'm in the beat of
Multiples and lies.
I'm in the beat of
I'm in the beat of
I'm in the beat of
Multiples and lies.

In the beginning there was the beginning
And the beginning began us.
Where there's water there's a thirsty beat
Needing more than water.
Where there's love there's a hungry lover
Dreaming of thirsty beats.
The Beat's my lover, he's thirsty water dreaming of beginning.

I'm in the beat of
I'm in the beat of
I'm in the beat of
Multiples and lies.
I'm in the beat of
I'm in the beat of
I'm in the beat of
Multiples and lies.
I'm in the beat of

I'm in the beat of
I'm in the beat of
Multiples and lies.
I'm in the beat of
I'm in the beat of
I'm in the beat of
Multiples and lies.
I'm in the beat of
I'm in the beat of
I'm in the beat of
Multiples and lies.
I'm in the beat of
I'm in the beat of
I'm in the beat of
Multiples and lies.

I'm in The Beast of multiples and lies.
In The Beast of promises and lies.
We were the beat of multiples and lies.

Rough Day

In August '09 I became a barman for six months in Manchester's finest gay bar, New York New York. These next two poems are from a sober drunk's perspective of drunks. That sober drunk is me, the barman. For barstaff everywhere . . . you know what I'm saying.

In one second of cheap vodka'd breath
You can scent a lifetime.
A purity
Consumed by the clarity of needing escape.
Each fuzzle-eyed guy
A story,
A laugh,
And accident waiting to hit and run on.

So many gay men have children,
So many of those children dead.
Some of them
Suicides or attempted,
Some of them doctors or drug dealers.
It's amazing the truths you're told.

Father Barman of Immaculate Inebriation,
Feeder of lost souls,
Hearer of drowned confessions.
Ancient disco and heart-felt ballads backdrop
And leave a melody behind the memory,
Lingering.

They fall in love with you,
The very old and the very young.
They flirt,
Ready to elope after a few scoops.
But most of all
They need you.

The man at the end of the bar
Is stood like an Easter Island statue,
Stony,
Peering forever forward.
I imagine he's forever facing the horror
Of not being beautiful.

The answer's not in the bottle
It's in the room;
The laughter of hen parties,
Howl of a wolf,
A song unsung
And the spill of a joke.
It's why they sing,
It's why they fight,
Why they love,
Growl,
And why they fuck.

There is a better world in chaos.
Try telling them there's not.
Throw up,
Not grow up,
And the granny whose lipstick misses her lips
Is queen mother to the camp explosion extolling her virtues.
He says if I were thirty years younger,
She says he still wouldn't stand a chance.
He dances too fast for her.
He dances like X-Factor.
She catches my eye,
Laughs.
Loves the cruelty.
Loves me laughing back.

I'm rushed off my feet.
Get to know the tippers.
Most tippers are sly,

Don't like it if they can't control you.
But they are tippers
And they do control you.

A straight bloke says if he was gay he'd fall for me.
I sell him poppers.
It won't be long before he falls
Out of love,
Out of favour,
And out of legs.
Blue-faced and spurting
Saturday's gibberish.
His missus whispers in my ear,
"I'm sure he's queer."

Blurred jamboree,
Ancient and forever.
E-heads dance the loudest.
I know most of them.
An old drunk queen
Kisses my forehead,
Says
This is better than medication.
It's the first thing he's said.
Starts raving with the E-heads.
They help him dance
Ecstatically.

I ache with the stomp of bass
And the fizz of cheap champagne.

Camp Me!

I loved working in that bar. A middle-aged treat. Its nickname was 'The Not Rite Bar'. It was where the not rights of gay society would booze and dance. A haven for the dying, the crying and the screaming. This is an amalgam of three of its customers.

A loud dead diva.
A gin brandy heroin
Hollerin' the last line
Like it could resurrect.

Wilde arms and boa tears.
Feathery spectacle of love gone mad
And long gone youth.
Stripped of paint and fancy dress.

Told ye!
Camp me!

Should see me in the mornin',
Head hangin' off a great night out,
Eyes the size of flyin' saucy,
Red as Bloody Marys.
Won't see me in a mirror today.

Camp me!
Told ye!

What did I say
And what did I sing?
I was Queen of the May . . .
Was I Queen of the May
Or up with the grannies again?

Round table friends,

Blackpool clowns,
Laughing like they're tumbling from planes.
Down!
Free-fall sprawl.
Every word I say hysterical.
Call me mental.

'Sisters, Sisters.'
Don't forget your parachutes.
'Never been such devoted sisters.'

Dodgems.
Bang! Bang!
Where's the gypsy who makes me spin faster?
The one who looks like Alan Bates.

I tripped and they were laughing.
Spilled my drink,
Broke my heel.

Warra my like?
Off me 'ead!

Told ye!
Camp me!

Wish I could speak well as I lip-sync,
Get it right every time.
Live alive the sound of mime.

'If there's a wrong way to do it,
A right way to screw it up.'

There are pictures in my head
And you're Victor Mature.
I'll be your tragedy,
Talk to me of love

And not much more.
Tell me I'm the only one,
Yours.
You'll never be gone.
Push a melon in my face
And lie.
C'mon, Jimmy Cagney,
Tell me it's all gonna be Yankee Doodle Dandy.
Tell me,

'Nobody does it like me.'
Nobody cat-walks it,
Lip-sync talks it.
'Nobody does it like me.'

Me!
Yeah,
Ye hear me say
Nobody does it like,
Nobody loves it like,
Nobody deserves it like,
Wears it like,
Tears it like
Meeeeeee!

No one liberates me like me.
Like camp me.

Warra my like!
Told ye!

Off me 'ead!
Me!

Jazz hands and broken heels.

YEAH!

Planet Middle Age

Hold your horses,
Your beer,
Hold all
You hold dear.
Hold your heart up to the sky,
Hold your tongue
Till language turns
To imagery.

Turn your radio on.

I'm up and around all this.
All over it,
Turned inside out like a well worn midnight.
Journeyed till the return is boring,
Tuned into yawning.
Taxi!
I'm seeing things in all their jaundiced glory:
A yellowed pageant of hackneyed history,
Pained;
A travelogue for the half-hearted
And restrained.

There's got to be a better cliché
Than going bald and grey.
Than the dawn of a brand new day.

I'm the old rock 'n' roll
Made now.
A shining tick tock
From the romantic '80s
And we all say in unison,
Like lemmings,
Eloquent lemmings,

Middle age is the new young.
We don't say in unison
I'm frightened.
We don't tell the truth.

We are the curse of positivia,
Dreams of insomnia.
We're the shorts
Where there used to be hot-pants.
Hot flushes
Where there used to be rants.

Planet Middle Age
And all its aliens
Are meant to be wise and friendly.
They're phases on stunning.

Is there life on Mars?
Is there any truth in the rumour
That you're still weak as a kitten,
Shaky as a blossom on a tree?
Planet Middle Age
And all its aliens
Are meant to be strong, tall,
And green.

It's the goodbyes
That ache,
Willow-speckled echoes
Of voices long gone.
Up to the sky,
Hidden in clouds,
If you please.

If there's a special place where echoes rain
Then build me a house with a leaky roof,
Get me a cat I can tell secrets to
And let it purr,

And let it pour.

My sister-in-law
Was the last of her family.
My home town, a dream.
Have I seen all there is?
Have I been all there is?

Planet Middle Age,
A show on *Radio Old*.
A repeat with a quizzical demographic
And I am and not quite tuned into
Its frequency.

It's all a bit jazz.
It's all a bit fast.
Flash!
Flash!
Flash!
Flash!
A splurge of tartan and hairspray,
A sprint through quicksand.
This glowing gold.

A hiccup in airwaves,
Idyll pornographic,
Car crash and urban.
A centrefold for the urbane.
A jog and a limp,
A cup of tea on speed,
Bumpy traffic.
Guinness and Bourbon.
This slowing down.

I'm old,
I'm in love
And young.
There's the rub.

Old.
Young.
And middle-aged.

Dream-Bound Inn

This is how I get drunk.

You're bound to dream in Dream-Bound Inn,
Because in Dream-Bound Inn
Shining stars with Darkness,
Both headliners on the same double bill.
They waltz,
Bright,
Quick-stepping the tangy musk of decades.
Such generous whores.

Infants age and crack,
Waiting for buses jammed with souls.
Don't all come at once.
Don't come at all.

Left by the log fire
Are tears being dried
So they, like tea-bags,
May be used again.
I hope there are eyes
Lucky enough to cry them
And spat sparks
Don't blind 'em.

I sit
And shadows pat my head
Like a toddler a dog,
Making sure I'm all there.
So affectionate and air-heavy,
They eat only sweet dreams.

Light catches face
And I've netted a fortune

In used-to-bes and always-wills.
Future's palpable glow,
Giving fast bucks
A run for their money.
Night stock
Catches.
I baulk at eternities
Waiting to grab my attention.

Monsters bleed away
Like the vanishing damp spots they are.
Out,
Damn monsters,
And the ugly you am.
Out,
Damn mothers.

I raise my glass to constant ghosts
Chattering good times,
And, loaded with a lopsided smile
And sheer bloody-mindlessness,
Toast fortune
To the instability of memories.
I sip,
Slip,
Wobble
Into the blessed-out knees-up ease
Of inebriate immortality.
"It's a poet's job to document legends,"
They slur,
"To find titanium in velvet."

Pockets Of Love

A middle-aged journey into night set in a nightclub. This verse monologue was first commissioned in 1989 for The Unity Theatre, Liverpool. I decided to write about a middle-aged gay man for whom the fruits of the gay scene had become out of reach. I performed the piece as well. I did this long before I was middle-aged and, my, does this piece hit home now.

One word can mean so much
Or so little.
Warm, giving ,
Harsh, brittle.
Hot palm,
Hand-killing cold,
Chilled intention hitting home.

For some it's a celebration of invitation,
Invitation into self.
But if you don't like who you are
You're inviting
Doubt, indecision
Crippling your decision,
Leaving you open to derision
From shadowed forms
You feel sure
Hope for your failure.

I saw your beauty
Silhouetted; first green, red, then blue.
Disco beat was fanfare
For your raven-black hair,
And the power of your stare
Led me straight to you.

I want to offer you welcome
Without breaking protection.

My barrier from your
Almost inevitable rejection.

If I don't try I'll never know.
This old adage brings me pain.
I take my life in my hands
And here I go again.

Palms sweat,
Eyes bleed as I approach.
I step from neon
Into multi-coloured darkness,
Music a minefield
Exploding in my head.
Snare drum times my step,
Heart beats a rhythm
A million drummers can't capture.

I stop.

Caught.
Out of time.
Fractured.
I realise it's my last chance to escape,
Limp into the arms and legs of a
Thudding, amyl nitrate-scented, dancefloor.
But that's not what I came for . . .
I want your sex so badly
It gives me strength to carry on
And, like Garland in *A Star Is Born*,
If I fail
I'll mourn you bravely
With a lament or song.

Maybe I could be wrong.

Fate might wear a new face,

A smile
Blessing my decision,
Condoning my direction.
Perhaps the chase has been worthwhile
And I won't be struck
By lust-sick diva blues.
If I'm in luck
We might just fuck.
So straighten up,
Right on in,
It's time to make the news.
That one word about to tumble from my lips.

"Hello. Is it me you're looking for?"

"NO!"

Well, I was easy to find.
No hide-and-seek
Or childish role-play here.
I was there for you,
You stupid bastard.
Whoever you were,
I was there.

Guess I'm not cut out to be
The paper doll you need.
Palms still clenched,
Eyes concede tears,
As seeing you walk away
Makes me stamp my feet and swear.

"Fuck!"

Much to the quiet amusement
Of the crowd around me.
I alter my face,

Smile without meaning,
Move back to my drink
Disguising the feeling of failure.

I know I'm not the sensitive lover
Displayed on stage and screen.
No soft-focused, silk-skinned, self-confessing,
Homoerotic, magazine-featured, drama queen.
I'm a little fat,
A touch round shouldered.
Not a public school boy
Or Venus in blue jeans.

But I'm real
Like the Moon,
Or the content of my briefs.
Sexual, huh?
But not to you.
You don't want anything less than perfection.
It's Cupid's bow and a dimple
You want caressing, your erection
Held aloft by a body of Olympian proportions.
These force-fed distortions sicken me
And ruin the chance of any real communication
Between two people.

Madonna chants empty expressions of love
As I leave the club,
Defeated,
By myself.
Not you,
Because just for tonight,
Just tonight,
I wanted perfection, too.

The warm air of this summer's evening,
Ice to my skin.

Humiliation turns to torment
As I begin
The same route home.
Same men fight,
Same women scream,
Same police harass,
Same people they've always been.
This circle of events is my weekend.
Can't pretend anything less,
Unless I try really hard.

Home provides coffee and a couch.
A safe haven for my withering mind.
A little bit of heaven
For the hacking insecurities
Hunting my head,
Crunching outside,
As I ask:
"Who will sooth the bruises of this already battered pride?"
Melodrama hits humour.
I laugh to break the fall
Before welts of depression
Cover me,
Blanket-bruising
Into despair.
I refuse to listen to those tortured divas
Who can't know my reality
And are far too dead to care.

My thoughts turn to you, lover,
Shadowed gladiator
In the gay arena.
I could turn you into Samson,
I could be Delilah.
Davina to your Goliath
Or Nero to your liar.
You scorch and sizzle

While I make do with a fiddle.
I'm a burning ember,
You're a raging fire,
A red hot teaser.
It's thumbs down for me
In these games,
Caesar.

Nobody's perfect.
Bet you wish they were.
Nobody's perfect.
That's why we get called queer.
Come rain or shine,
Shower or storm,
I'm aware of that.
Proud.
When I'm cold,
Wear it like a coat.
It sometimes weighs me down
To my knees,
Forced to the ground
By my pockets of love.

Love to share in many forms.
Wham bam thank you ma'am.
A fine rap for me, lover,
Or a long romance
If you fit the bill, lover.
But whatever the weather,
I'll weather the weather,
Whether I like it or not,
Because I will never be your lover,
Lover.

Your pockets seemed empty,
Room only for money.
Currency to perfection.

You're still out there,
Cruising for a bruising,
Hovering, manoeuvring.
Until, after much inspection,
You'll home in on the boy
With the tightest arse,
Widest smile.
After a while
Offer drink;
Ambrosia your martyr,
Nectar your saint.
A loving cup of deception.

You'll be so good at the tales you weave,
A craftsman of care, compliment and intrigue.
The boy will believe he's the only one.
You smile, content at a job well done,
The night has only just begun
For you and your endeavour.
A secret agent under cover,
Cascading nonsense.
Handsome fool,
Pouring words, blood from a wound,
Spewing forth your offer.
Showering lies
Like the best of spies
On your one-night lover.

And it should've been me! Wo ho ho . . .
It should've been me!

I think I'm jealous.
I don't feature in your magazines.
Mr Normal, no imagery,
Stepping invisibly
From scene to scene.

I can't use beauty as bait,
Haven't the face to kiss a thousand lips.
My body isn't my battle cry,
A built up, worked on, fantasy
Of bulging pecks, slender hips.

You could have tried, lover,
To be bigger than that glossy deceit.
This has come too late,
You're content with your conceit.
Narcissus and his playmate.

And me?
Not even a runner-up in the good looks stakes.